the series on school reform

Patricia A. Wasley
Bank Street College of Education

Ann Lieberman
NCREST

Joseph P. McDonald
New York University

Series Editors

Looking Together at
Student Work

A COMPANION GUIDE TO
Assessing Student Learning

Tina Blythe
David Allen
Barbara Schieffelin Powell

Teachers College, Columbia University
New York and London

Published by Teachers College Press, 1234 Amsterdam Avenue, New York, NY 10027

Library of Congress Cataloging-in-Publication Data
  Blythe, Tina, 1964–
    Looking together at student work: a companion guide to Assessing student learning / Tina Blythe, David Allen, Barbara Schieffelin Powell.
      p.   cm. — (The series on school reform)
    Includes bibliographic references (p.   ).
    ISBN 0-8077-3855-7 (pbk.: alk. paper)
    1. Grading and marking (Students)—United States. 2. Educational tests and measurements—United States.   I. Allen, David, 1961–   II. Powell, Barbara Schieffelin.   III. Assessing student learning.   IV. Title.   V. Series
  LB3051 .B54 1999
  371.27—dc21   99-22561

ISBN 0-8077-3855-7 (paper)

Printed on acid-free paper

Manufactured in the United States of America

06 05 04 03 02 01   8 7 6 5 4 3

Contents

❖ Foreword ❖

Across the country and abroad, school reformers have recognized the pressing need to place actual student work formally and respectfully at the center of both public and private conversations about school. From California to Vermont, from school reform organizations to their many working partners in schools, teaching centers, and universities, people are trying out new tools for making change through that most radical of activities: unarmed discussion.

When people who come at school change with very different beliefs and assumptions meet to look at student work, their mutual understanding often deepens. Using diplomatic protocols that make communication feel "safe," they often find common ground and can move more surely toward creating the conditions in which teachers and students might do better throughout the system.

Though these tools differ, all share a focus on bringing together people across the school community—teachers, parents, students, and outside visitors—to look at student work. All aim to learn something that will then affect future teaching and learning, not just the individual student whose work they examine. And all provide a formal structure, or "protocol," that, while often uncomfortable at first, surfaces and values different points of view.

David Allen has compared such protocols to putting on a play, "though the dialogue," he notes, "is mainly improvisational." Yet just as theatrical styles that range from classical to "method" can all work magic on the mind and the soul, effective protocols have their styles and purposes, too.

Some fall on the more evaluative end of the spectrum, aiming to analyze and thus improve teaching strategies and curriculum. Others rely more on close description to heighten teachers' understanding of individual children and hence affect teacher practice. Some look at a moment in time and extend its meaning outward; others take an accumulated body of evidence and draw new meanings from its larger picture.

Thoughtful, rigorous, and user-friendly, this book lays out some of the best ways to go about this process. Any group of teachers, parents, or community members could use it to participate in the hard work of assessing where our schools are and how they can improve.

Once begun, that cycle of reflecting together on direct evidence, drawing out its meaning, and then folding what we learn back into the daily work may prove the very engine of school change in the critical years ahead. "I used to think student work was between student and teacher," one teacher told me recently. "Now I think all work should be as public, and as shared, as possible." When a teacher can say that, things have begun to move. This book will help.

Kathleen Cushman

❖ Authors' Note ❖

This guide is a companion to *Assessing Student Learning: From Grading to Understanding* (Teachers College Press, 1998). It is intended to provide teachers with strategies and resources for working together to examine and discuss student work—science projects, essays, art work, math problems, and more. To give some real examples of the ways teachers do this, we describe the two structured conversations, or protocols, we know best: the Collaborative Assessment Conference and the Tuning Protocol. We do *not* describe other valuable protocols, including the Descriptive Review processes, Primary Language Record, California Protocol, and Roundtables. For more information about these, as well as the Collaborative Assessment Conference and Tuning Protocol, see appropriate chapters of *Assessing Student Learning* and the materials included on the list of resources in this volume.

A Note About Terminology. The strategies and process we describe in this book are appropriate for teachers of all grades (K–12, and beyond). We use the term "student" for children and adolescents in all grades. We use the term "student work" to refer to things students produce, usually in response to a teacher's assignment. The terms "protocol," "process," and "structure" are all applied to facilitated conversations about student work that involve multiple steps and guidelines for participation.

Acknowledgments. As we developed this book, many people shared with us their ideas about and experiences with looking collaboratively at student work. For this help, we thank the teachers and administrators of Charles Shaw Middle School, Gorham, Maine; the teachers and administrators of Rosemont Middle School, Norfolk, Virginia; the teachers and administrators of North Shore High School and Manhasset High School (Long Island); and the members of the "Student Work" Working Group of the ATLAS Seminar.

In particular, we acknowledge the important contributions of the following teachers and administrators: John Caterina, Jean Davis, Colleen

Fleming, Diane Knott, Jane Montagna, John Newlin, Evelyn Ort, Vicki Pearce, Jim Silcox, and Nancy Young.

Many thanks to Eric Buchovecky, Thomas Hatch, Sara Hendren, and Steven Levy, who provided us with detailed comments on earlier manuscripts.

This book is a product of the ATLAS Seminar, which was funded by the Spencer Foundation, the John D. and Catherine T. MacArthur Foundation, and the Rockefeller Foundation. We are grateful for their generous support.

❖ CHAPTER 1 ❖

Introduction

The faculty of a recently founded charter high school in Massachusetts realized that their new school community needed to develop a shared set of standards for evaluating student work. To begin that process, they planned a 3-hour afternoon session to which they invited parents, students, and the entire staff of the school. At that session, everyone examined and discussed the same 10 pieces of student writing. In small groups, they answered three questions: Which of these pieces is the strongest and why? Which of these pieces is the weakest and why? Which would we expect a 7th/10th/12th grader to be able to write?

In Virginia, a middle school had just made exhibitions (public presentations of students' long-term research projects) a requirement for students at three grade levels. The faculty needed a way to train people from outside the school to serve as judges on exhibition panels. To accomplish this goal, they designed a training session around discussing videotaped examples of student exhibitions. The judges-in-training looked at the examples and talked together about how they would have responded if they had been judges on those exhibition panels. Looking together at the student work gave them the opportunity to think through what it means to be a judge before they had to assume that role themselves.

When a middle school in Maine began using portfolio assessment, the faculty wanted to involve students and parents in examining the work collected in the portfolios to see whether it demonstrated progress toward the students' goals for the year. The faculty and students designed a conferencing system that brought parents, student, and teacher together twice a year to review and discuss the work in each student's portfolio.

Although their situations differ, these schools share three important features:

- Each school was in the midst of important changes in the way student work was structured, presented, and/or assessed.
- Each school had identified a particular goal that it needed to accomplish in order to carry out the changes.
- Each school used the strategy of looking collaboratively at student work as a way of moving toward its goal.

This book is based on work done in these schools and others like them. It is designed for schools and teachers of all grade levels. If one or more of the following descriptions fits you and your colleagues, you may find the ideas in this book especially helpful:

- You already use projects, exhibitions, or portfolios, and you want to make them more effective learning tools for your students.
- You are trying a new teaching approach or learning activity in your classroom(s) and want to look more closely at its impact on your students' work.
- You are looking for ways to talk more often and more thoughtfully with your colleagues about teaching, learning, and assessment.
- You are looking for ways to reflect on, discuss with others, and revise your own practice.
- You are looking for ways to talk with the broader community outside the school about the teaching, learning, and assessment going on inside your school.

What Does This Book Do?

This book is designed to provide educators (teachers, administrators, curriculum coordinators, staff developers, and others) with resources for working together to examine and discuss student work—projects, art work, essays, and other products of class assignments. These products provide the most important evidence of student growth and learning and of the effectiveness of teachers' own practices. The resources in this book include:

- A process for starting and sustaining collaborative discussions of student work
- Descriptions of two established structures, or "protocols," for guiding discussion of student work: the Tuning Protocol and the Collaborative Assessment Conference
- Examples from schools that have developed their own ways of talking about student work
- A list of resources (books, articles, videos, and organizations) that can provide further help

What Doesn't This Book Do?

This book does not provide a recipe for how your school should look at and talk about student work. Nor does it provide you with a list of questions that you should use when looking at student work. Only you and the people with whom you work know the needs and goals of your faculty, community, and students. The models provided here can give you a starting point, but the questions and the specific process you use must be identified by those involved in that process.

It does not give detailed information about how to do exhibitions, project work, portfolios, or any of the other kinds of tasks that are typically the focus of such collaborative discussions. However, the resource list at the end of the book can direct you to further reading about these topics.

It does not tell you how to develop standards, criteria, or rubrics for student work, although you could decide to use one or more of the processes described in this book to serve that purpose.

It does not provide a blueprint for the structural changes that may accompany a school's efforts to support discussions of student work. However, you will find some practical suggestions in various chapters of the book to help you to develop such a plan.

How Do Teachers Usually Look at Student Work?

Teachers have always spent a good deal of time looking at student work. They read it in order to provide feedback to the students who did it. They look at student work in order to evaluate it, assigning it a score or a grade. They examine it for clues about how to plan future curricula and assessments that will best serve the students, or to prepare for parent conferences. Many teachers consider the process of examining, assessing, and evaluating student work one of the most important—and time-consuming—aspects of their work. Most of this work is done by teachers individually, alone at their desks in classrooms, at their kitchen tables, even waiting in doctors' offices or at their children's basketball practice.

Why Look at Student Work Collaboratively?

Looking collaboratively at student work is not meant to replace the important ways you look at student work by yourself. However, working with others can bring to the surface resources, ideas, and strategies that make the individual efforts more productive. It is hard to imagine doctors who never consult with other physicians (or with their patients) but rather make all decisions about their patients' prognoses and treatments on their own. Like doctors, educators also benefit from consultation with colleagues. In the teaching profession, student work provides the data that allow professionals to work together to make the best possible decisions for their students.

In addition, there are some purposes for looking at student work that virtually *require* collaboration and conversation—developing common standards within grade levels or departments, for example. In order to accomplish this aim, a school or a group of teachers must develop not only the standards but also a shared understanding of what those standards mean and how to apply them to students' work. Examining and discussing samples of student work is virtually the only way to achieve such a goal.

How Many People Does It Take to "Look Together"?

Sometimes, "looking together" means that a whole school is engaged in a particular process or strategy for examining student work. More often, such collaboration begins with a small group of teachers—typically from two or three to seven or eight—who have a common interest: They want to find out more about the kinds of problems that fourth graders are having in math. Or they want to consider how to improve the eleventh grade writing course. Or they want to get ideas from one another about how to manage and assess portfolios in their classrooms. One person in the group serves as facilitator, a role we discuss in Chapter 2.

How Much Time Does It Take to Hold Collaborative Discussions of Student Work?

More time than it takes to look at a single piece of student work by yourself. How much more depends on your group's particular goals for looking at the work, and on the process you use. Some goals (establishing common standards about student work, for example) may take only one or two sessions a year. Other goals (such as finding out more about the learning styles and needs of individual students) require more frequent meetings—anywhere from once a week to once a month to four or five times a year. The duration of these meetings also varies according to their purpose. Typical meetings last from 45 minutes to an hour and a half. Some schools have benefited from half- or full-day meetings focused on examining student work.

Finding this kind of time is not easy. Schools are not typically structured to support teacher collaboration: Rigid bell schedules, limited planning time, and the sheer number of students in a single teacher's load all work against thoughtful and productive collaboration. Nor has teaching developed some of the forms of evidence-based collaboration typical of other professions—consultations with colleagues, case reviews, and conferences. Indeed, it is unusual for anybody besides the teacher, the student, and occasionally a parent to examine any given piece of that student's work, let alone to comment on it or raise questions about it or learn from it.

Why Use a "Protocol"?

Why not just start talking? Protocols, such as the Collaborative Assessment Conference and the Tuning Protocol, provide structures for conversations about student work. They ask participants, including the presenter, to go through a number of steps in a fixed order. For example, in the Tuning Protocol, the teacher's presentation is followed by "clarifying questions" from other participants. Such structures prompt participants to offer certain kinds of comments (such as descriptions, questions, or judgments). While some people find protocols artificial, at least at first, our experience and research suggest that the structure for the conversation provides a safe, supportive environment for teachers to share publicly their students' work and their own—something they don't typically do. Protocols also encourage other teachers to offer substantive feedback to their colleague(s)—again, something that doesn't happen often in teachers' lives. They provide teachers with a time and a forum for individual and group reflection on student work, student learning, and their own teaching. They help avoid quick judgments about student work. With so many pressing concerns competing for teachers' time, the protocols help stay focused on the essentials of teaching and learning for at least 45 minutes at a time. In the hurly-burly of teaching, this is both a luxury and a necessity.

In Summary

Much will have to change about schooling as we know it to support a truly collaborative working environment for teachers. But even without fundamental changes, some teachers and administrators have begun to find ways to work together to look at and learn from samples of student work. In writing this book, we have drawn on the experiences of some of these teachers, as well as those of the facilitators, university educators, and researchers who have worked with them. The book's goal is to support all educators as they develop their own models of professional collaboration.

❖ CHAPTER 2 ❖

Developing a Way of Looking Together at Student Work

Teaching well is really a cyclical process. It requires setting goals, planning, and continuous evaluation and adjustment, as well as the interaction with students that is its heart. Examining student work is an important and complex part of teaching, yet there are few resources to support it. The steps that follow are offered as one such resource. They describe how some groups of teachers have begun to examine their students' work collaboratively. These steps include:

1. Taking stock of current ways of looking at student work
2. Establishing goals and framing questions
3. Choosing, adapting, or developing a process for looking collaboratively at student work
4. Implementing the process
5. Reflecting on and revising the process

Like teaching itself, this process is not linear, but cyclical. When teachers reach the last step, in which they reflect on and revise the process, they go back to the beginning with a better understanding of what they're looking for and how to look. Figure 2.1 represents this process.

Although experiences differ for every group of teachers that undertakes a collaborative examination of student work, some commonalties emerge. For each of the steps, we have offered some lessons from teachers' experiences: what to watch for and what to watch out for. We have also included some very brief examples or "snapshots" from schools engaged in looking at student work.

Taking Stock of Current Ways of Looking at Student Work

Schools never start from scratch in collaboratively examining student work. Teachers have always looked individually at their students' work to

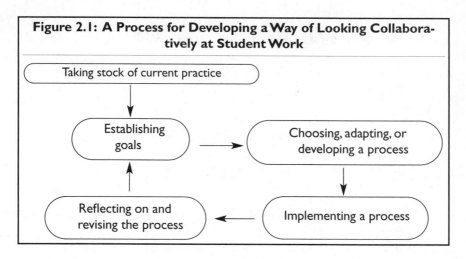

Figure 2.1: A Process for Developing a Way of Looking Collaboratively at Student Work

Taking stock of current practice

Establishing goals

Choosing, adapting, or developing a process

Reflecting on and revising the process

Implementing a process

assess student achievement and progress. In planning to work collaboratively, it is useful to look for examples of how teachers currently examine student work and to consider how these ways might be adapted or expanded. For example, if students regularly make public presentations of their project work to parents and classmates, teachers might arrange to attend these presentations and then to discuss them afterward. Taking stock of current practices can bring to the surface some of the questions and issues that are not addressed by how student work is currently treated.

> In one elementary school, each student traditionally met regularly with her teacher to work on a set of math problems. These conferences formed part of each child's math portfolio that was used for assessment purposes. At these meetings, the student had the list of problems in front of her; the teacher sat across the table and noted how she worked the problems, sometimes asking the student questions about how she had done her work. "We're not just interested in whether they got the answer right, but how. Do they use their fingers? Work on scratch paper? Ask for help?" One teacher decided to videotape the conferences. When the faculty as a whole began meeting to look at students' math work, the videotapes provided a particularly effective focus for teachers' discussions about teaching math problem-solving and individualizing instruction.

❖❖ *What to Watch For.* In what ways do you (and others within your school) currently examine student work either individually or collaboratively? (For example, do you review portfolios together or sit in on each other's student exhibitions?)

❖❖ There may be resistance to trying a new way of looking at student work with other teachers, especially if people in the school are used to their own ways of doing so. Is the new process meeting a genuine need? Does it allow everyone to enter into a new approach in a way that is comfortable for them?

Establishing Goals and Framing Questions

The purposes for examining and discussing student work are many and varied. Some common ones include:

- Learning more about an individual child's response to an assignment
- Setting standards for all students' performances
- Learning about your own teaching and assessment practices
- Honing observational and interpretive skills

Being clear about the purpose for looking at student work will help your group to select the most appropriate process or guide the group in developing its own. (It is not always easy—indeed, not always possible—to articulate goals at the beginning of a process. At the end of this chapter, we offer an alternative to starting off with well-articulated goals.)

Broad goals, like the four mentioned above, are usually established through conversations prior to engaging in the examination of student work. In these preliminary conversations, teachers address questions like:

- What are the crucial teaching and learning issues in our school now?
- What do we need more information about (in addition to the information that test scores and grades typically provide)?

These conversations might take place within a teaching team, at a department meeting, or within a study group. Often, one person on the faculty acts as the catalyst, calling a group's attention to the opportunity for learning afforded by looking together at student work. In other cases, collaboratively examining student work may be an explicit part of a school's strategy for professional development and school improvement.

The faculty of a new small high school with a bilingual student body struggled with how to make language development a focus for the whole school: how to get all teachers involved in teaching reading, writing, and speaking. One teacher asked, "What if we have students keep language portfolios in their Humanities class, but when it comes to evaluating them, involve the entire faculty and administration in reading and responding to them? Then when we come together in team meetings we can look at the portfolios and the response letters we write to students, and really talk about our students' language development and what we're doing to support it." Here, the school's goal was clear: making language development more central to the work of the faculty. Looking at student work (by collectively examining and discussing students' language portfolios) became one tool for accomplishing that goal.

In order to achieve the initial agreement, participants must be open to other perspectives, listen to each other, and discuss individual interests and concerns. But reaching initial agreement is just the beginning: Determining the broad goals for looking collaboratively at student work should be a cyclical process, in which participants agree on their questions, get involved in addressing those questions by looking at student work, and emerge with greater clarity about the questions, leading them to revise the initial question or to articulate others.

Once you have an idea of the broad area of concern, it is important to narrow the focus. Many teachers have found it helpful to frame one or two "focusing questions"—questions that help the group concentrate on a particular aspect of the student work and/or assignment being presented. The most important questions usually come from the teacher or teachers who actually present their students' work for collaborative examination but are strongly related to school-wide questions and broad concerns of the faculty.

Carolyn, a high school English teacher, had assigned a large-scale independent research project for the first time. She struggled with the widely varied quality of the papers that her students produced. Her department had recently set aside time once a month to look at student work collaboratively as one way to support the department members in the ongoing development of their teaching skills. When Carolyn brought in her students' papers for the group to look at, she also brought a focusing question: "How can I provide supportive, individualized instruction without taking away from students' ownership of their topics and their learning about independent research?"—a focusing question that dovetailed with the group's broader goal of helping one another to improve teaching.

There are probably as many types of questions as there are teachers. Figure 2.2 describes some categories of questions that you may want to consider as you move from the group's broad questions to framing your own more specific ones for examining student work.

**Figure 2.2: Kinds of Questions That Might Guide
the Examination of Student Work**

About the quality of student work:

- Is the work good enough?
- What is "good enough"?
- In what ways does this work meet or fail to meet a particular set of standards?

About teaching practice:

- What do the students' responses indicate about the effectiveness of the prompt or assignment? How might the assignment be improved?
- What kinds of instruction support high quality student performances?

About students' understanding:

- What does this work tell us about how well the student understands the topic of the assignment?
- What initial understandings do we see beginning to emerge in this work?

About students' growth:

- How does this range of work from a single student demonstrate growth over time?
- How can I support student growth more effectively?

About students' intent:

- What issues or questions is this student focused on?
- What aspects of the assignment intrigued this student?
- Into which parts of the assignment did the student put the most effort?
- To what extent is the student challenging herself? In what ways?

❖ *What to Watch For.* Is your group agreeing on one or two clearly stated, broader purposes for examining student work? If the group has articulated focusing questions, can they be addressed by looking at student work?

❖ Are there too many purposes on the table for the group to focus on, instead of one or two? Do members of the group seem to have fundamentally different ideas about the purposes for looking at student work? Do the questions you want to ask seem marginal (too small) or unanswerable (too large)?

An Alternative Approach. Getting clear about purpose is not always straight-forward or easy. Within every school exist different—sometimes compet-ing—perspectives on teaching and learning goals and methods. If the group is unsure of its goals or is in danger of spending too much time trying to come to initial agreement, you might want to use the "let's-try-it-and-see-what-happens" approach. Rather than articulating specific goals initially, your group can decide to make the initial goal very general—perhaps even vague.

For example, several teachers might decide that they would like a lit-tle more time for reflecting on what is happening in their classrooms. Or they might decide that they would like to have more structure for their conversations during faculty meetings or in team planning time. Looking collaboratively at student work would be a way to accomplish either of these very general goals.

Inevitably, the process of looking together at student work raises a host of thoughts, questions, and concerns. From these issues that emerge over successive uses of the process, the group members may be able to articulate more crisply and specifically the goals they would like to pursue. They could then decide to refine the process they are using in order to achieve those goals more effectively, or they might decide that such goals require an entirely different process and adopt or develop one of their own.

Choosing, Adapting, or Developing a Process for Looking Collaboratively

Once you have established (more or less) the purposes for examining stu-dent work together or have articulated questions to explore, you can iden-tify a process that will help you achieve your ends. A number of such processes are currently in use. Two of them are described in detail in Chap-ter 4 of this book. They are:

- *The Tuning Protocol:* Developed by Joseph McDonald and colleagues in the early 1990s for the Coalition of Essential Schools, the Tuning Proto-col is a structured, facilitated conversation that asks participants to pro-vide the presenting teacher(s) with feedback—both "warm" and "cool"—on a project, task, or exhibition. At the heart of the process is an examination of student work samples.
- *The Collaborative Assessment Conference:* The Collaborative Assessment Conference was developed in 1988 by Steve Seidel and colleagues at Harvard Project Zero. The Collaborative Assessment Conference in-vites teachers to look at, describe, and ask questions about pieces of

student work in order to develop a deeper understanding of the student who created it, of that student's interests and strengths, and of the teaching/learning environment.

Other processes currently used include:

- *The Consultancy Process,* developed at the Coalition of Essential Schools
- *The Descriptive Review of the Child,* developed by Patricia Carini at the Prospect Center in Vermont
- *The Primary Language Record,* developed in 1985 by the Centre for Language in Primary Education in London

Resources listed in the appendix of this book can help you learn more about these and other processes for looking collaboratively at student work.

Although these and other processes differ in practical ways (the size of the group for which they are appropriate, the number of samples of student work they typically have as their focus, and so on), there are two crucial aspects to which you should pay particular attention as you choose or develop a process:

- *Mode of looking,* or the degree to which the process encourages participants to "describe," "interpret," or "evaluate" the work being presented. Some processes emphasize description, others, evaluation.
- *Context,* or the way and extent to which the process makes room for presentation of the work's context (background information about the student who created the work, the assignment and conditions under which it was carried out, and so on). Some processes begin with the teacher-presenter describing the context; some call for the teacher to present the context after the group has examined the work; in other processes, the context is never presented.

More than any other factors, these two elements will influence the flavor of the group's conversation, the kinds of issues that emerge during the conversation, and the kinds of goals the conversation will enable the group to reach. In Chapter 3, we consider these two aspects of design in more detail.

❖❖ **What to Watch For.** Has the group discussed the choice of process? (Starting with an already-established process, rather than immediately developing your own, can be helpful; however, deciding exactly which process is the right one to start with may not be easy.)

❖❖ After using a particular protocol a few times, the group may discuss other processes they want to try. Is there agreement about trying a new process? Has the original process the group began with been given a fair try? (The group may need to try a process several times before participants can tell how well it is helping them move toward their goals.)

Implementing a Process

No matter which process you use, you will need to address important practical issues in order to carry out that process. We have divided these issues into two categories:

- Key Questions
- Logistics

Key Questions

Who Will Be Involved in the Process? Participants might include teachers, administrators, parents, students, colleagues from other schools, and representatives from the community (such as teachers from local colleges, community leaders, and business people). Other options include deciding whether to organize groups within or across grade levels, subject areas, and/or schools in the district. Teachers may naturally want to keep the discussion "within the family." For some purposes this makes good sense, but consider what might be learned from informed and sympathetic outsiders.

> We always learn more when we involve different people in looking at student work. It may take more effort to organize those meetings, but the result is always of higher quality.
>
> —High school principal

Who Will Present Student Work? Every teacher can learn from presenting, but no one should be forced to present. Some teachers will be more comfortable than others in presenting their students' work. Pairs or teams of teachers may present together, and often this approach reduces stress for the presenting team. If the idea of presenting your student work seems daunting, it may help to remember that the structure of the process and the facilitation will create a safe atmosphere to talk about issues related to practice. In any case, the presentation should be seen as conversational rather than rehearsed.

I was nervous about presenting my students' work, but as soon as people started talking, I could relax, because they saw the good things about my kids and
they helped me see some things I could do differently.

—High school special education teacher

What Kind of Student Work Will Be Presented? The kind of student work
presented will best be determined by the purposes and questions you
define. Particular processes, too, may lend themselves to different kinds of
work. For example, the Collaborative Assessment Conference is often
used with a single piece of work, and the Tuning Protocol for examination
of multiple samples. Whatever process you use, here are some issues for
the presenting teacher (in consultation with the facilitator) to consider in
choosing student work:

- *Work that piques your curiosity:* Choosing a piece or collection of
  student work about which you have a genuine question will help
  to ensure a productive conversation. Is there a piece or body of
  student work that raises a question for you? Are you wondering
  how to improve an assignment that was not particularly success-
  ful? Would you like others' perspectives on the work of a student
  you feel you do not understand or appreciate as well as you
  would like to? Check with the facilitator about when and how you
  should share your questions with the group.
- *Number of pieces of work:* Do you want to look at a single piece of
  work? Several drafts of a single piece? Several pieces from different students? Several pieces from the same student? Again, it will
  be helpful to consult with the facilitator in making this decision,
  since he or she will have a feel for the kind and amount of work
  best served by the process you will be using.
- *Quality or level of the work:* Do you want to share a polished piece, a
  rough draft, or perhaps several drafts and the finished piece? Do
  you want to bring the very best piece of the batch or a piece that
  fell short of your expectations?
- *Context for the work:* How much context is called for by the protocol in which you will be participating? If the process is one in
  which the work's context is shared, you might want to make some
  notes for yourself about what you want to say. (Review the
  process schedule or check with the group facilitator to find out
  how much time you'll have to say it.) You might want to describe
  the objectives for the assignment, the amount of time the students
  had to carry it out, how the project or task was organized, the
  evaluation criteria, and so on. Bring copies of any context-related

documents (the assignment sheet, the scoring rubric, description of objectives) that you might want to share with the group.

- *Sharing the work in the meeting:* How will everyone in the group be able to examine the work? Discuss this in advance with the facilitator so that the two of you can work out the logistics ahead of time. Figure 2.3 offers some suggestions for making different kinds of work easily accessible for group examination.

What About Students' Rights to Confidentiality? Respecting students' ownership of their work and their right to control who sees it and how it is used is essential. Typically, students produce schoolwork assuming that only their teacher (and perhaps a few classmates or family members) will see it. For sharing student work within the school, the faculty and administration should establish a policy that addresses confidentiality issues. (Such a policy might include, for example, asking the students' permission to share their work. Students often appreciate the fact that you take

---

Figure 2.3: Making Student Work Accessible for Group Examination: Tips for the Presenting Teacher

Written work: Try to have copies for everyone, especially if the piece is longer than a page. If you do not have copies and the writing is brief, you might try reading it out loud two or three times for the group. For especially long pieces, you might want to focus only on particular sections. You might also invite different group members to examine different sections of a longer work and then to describe it for the whole group.

Two-dimensional art work: If the art work is small, try to make copies. If the art work is in color and the copies are black-and-white, bring the original with you so that people can refer to it for more detail.

Three-dimensional work: For posterboard displays, dioramas, models, and similar kinds of three-dimensional work, set up the piece in a central location where all the participants can see it. If the group is large, it might be useful to set it up just before the meeting, so that participants can have a chance to examine it closely while they are waiting for the meeting to begin.

Video: If you want to show a video of student work, choose the clip carefully—a 5- to 7-minute piece is usually as much as a group can work with in a typical 1- to 2-hour meeting. The group may need to see the clip twice in order to discuss the student work in detail. (A transcript can be helpful.) Be sure to let the facilitator know ahead of time that you want to use video so that she can arrange to have video equipment at the meeting.

their work seriously enough to want to discuss it with other teachers. They also may want to hear something about what other people had to say about it.)

If you plan to take the work outside of the school building, it is a good idea to ask the student and/or the parent or guardian (depending on the age of the student) to sign a release form that gives permission for the work to be shared publicly. If you have no way of obtaining permission from the student or the parents, remove the student's name from the work and take every precaution not to reveal his or her identity in the course of the conversation. (You may want to take this step even if you have the student's and parent's or guardian's permission.)

Remember that using video or photographs of children raises important confidentiality concerns.

Logistics

When Will You Meet? If the examination of student work is to become a regular practice, how can it be given a regular slot in the school's schedule? Can groups meet to look at student work on release days? During team planning time? During department meetings or study group meetings? Assess how meeting time is currently used. What could be handled in another way (for example, printing a set of announcements for everyone rather than spending twenty minutes of a meeting reading them out loud) so that examining student work can take place?

It is important that teachers find not only enough time but also the right time:

> So much depends on the particular day when people can meet. We did a Tuning Protocol before a long weekend that was much better than in the middle of the week. . . . Or we meet in the evening when people can have dinner.
>
> —High school teacher

Where Will You Meet? Teachers' room, classroom, auditorium? Since most meetings involve ten or fewer participants, it makes sense to look for a comfortable space with enough room to spread out materials—and equipment, such as video players—but not so much that the group feels dwarfed.

> We used to use a classroom after school, but then for some reason we had to find a new place. We moved to the band room. Something about being in a different space, a more special one, made a big difference.
>
> —Middle school teacher and group leader

Who Will Facilitate? All the processes described in this book require a facilitator, someone to keep the group focused on the task and make sure the structure and guidelines of the process are followed. Everyone can learn to facilitate, but not everyone will feel comfortable doing so, especially the first few times the group meets. It takes practice as well as cooperation from the full group. Some groups have found it helpful to have a facilitator from outside the group, at least for the first few times. Some groups rotate facilitation among themselves. (See Figure 2.4 for more suggestions about facilitation.)

> I learned a lot about teaching from facilitating meetings. I think it's important for the facilitator to stay in that role, even if he's dying to jump in with comments or questions for the presenting teacher. The group needs somebody who can make sure everybody is heard.
>
> —Middle school teacher

❖❖ **What to Watch For.** As you begin to talk about the student work, unforeseen issues and questions will arise. You may start out looking at how a student's work rates on the criteria or rubric and shift to discussing whether the rubric is adequate for the kinds of work students are producing. Such issues are important, and discovering them is one of the great benefits of looking collaboratively at student work. On the other hand, it is easy to start out talking about a student's work and end up talking about something incidental (for example, a field trip the student's class recently took). The facilitator and the group must decide whether these emergent issues or questions should be discussed immediately or noted for later attention.

❖❖ The protocol that guides the conversation should help the group to keep to its stated goals and focusing questions. However, if you are facilitating, be aware that some people may react negatively to the artificial structure that such a protocol imposes on the discussion. It is useful to recognize this but not to give up on the structure the group has decided upon. Instead, go through the process as planned and save time afterwards for a debriefing discussion (see "Reflecting on and Revising the Process" below). Often, discussion with colleagues helps those who are most critical of the structure to see its value.

Reflecting on and Revising the Process

After looking at student work collaboratively, groups need time to reflect on and discuss two questions:

Figure 2.4: Three Suggestions for Facilitators

Have an agenda. If the agenda has not already been developed when the meeting begins, spend a few minutes with the group developing one. Make sure everyone has a copy or that it is posted in a prominent place. Review it aloud at the beginning of the meeting, reiterate the goals of the process, and then help people to stick to the agenda during the meeting. Discussing student work is a very thought-provoking process. It raises diverse and complex issues for the people involved in it. In order to keep the discussion focused, you may need to provide reminders about the topic or question currently on the table or about the time limit for a given portion of the schedule. Inviting everyone to share the responsibility for keeping the conversation on track will make your job easier.

Try not to participate in the substance of the conversation. It is very easy to get caught up in a discussion and to lose track of facilitation duties, such as making sure everyone has a chance to speak, sticking to agreed-upon time limits, and so on. Although it is not impossible for one person to act as both facilitator and participant, it is probably not a good starting place for a novice facilitator. If no one in the group wants to give up the chance to be an active talker in the conversation, you might consider inviting a person from outside the group to facilitate the meeting.

Maintain a nonjudgmental attitude. The success of any process for looking at student work is dependent on the group's ability to share their thoughts honestly and respectfully. It is a good idea to remind group members at the beginning of a session about the need for respect and sensitivity in their comments, and then to model that consideration in your own interactions with the group. Criticism from you about participants' comments or about the presenting teacher's work will prevent a conversation of any depth from developing. Even comments that imply a positive assessment ("Excellent point!") are judgments nonetheless and can have a similar effect.

On the other hand, respectfully accepting all contributions may encourage people to speak honestly. For instance, responding to an ambiguous comment with, "Could you explain a little more about what you mean?" is more helpful than "That's confusing" or "That's off the topic." "Respectful acceptance" does not mean that you have to sit by idly while the comments wander further and further afield from the agenda, but rather that care should be used in redirecting participants to the agreed-upon topic or schedule.

- What are we learning through this process?
- How can the process be improved so that it helps us to achieve our goal(s) more effectively?

What Are We Learning Through This Process? When teachers meet to look at and discuss student work, everybody learns. Sometimes the lessons are very direct: "Now I know how to work with students on this particular problem." Often, though, teachers' learning is more general: "I see the need to be much clearer with students about the criteria." Much of this learning becomes personal as teachers (the presenter as well as others) reflect on what they have learned through the process about their own students, standards, and practice.

> A high school teachers' group on Friday afternoon had just completed a process focused on examining student research papers. The teachers' reflections on the session revealed the variety in what they had learned from it. The presenting teacher commented, "There is so much out there on the table now for me to think about, like what you [another teacher in the group] said about audience." Another teacher made the connection to her own practice: "I'm thinking about my science investigations with students and this whole issue of how much to intervene."

How Can the Process Be Improved So That It Helps Us to Achieve Our Goal(s) More Effectively? It is also important for participants to consider what they have learned about the process for examining student work itself: What worked? What should change? Is this the right process for the group's goals? In some cases, answering these questions will lead to changing the process or developing a new process.

As your group gets more familiar with a particular process through repeated use, you might consider loosening the structure a bit. There is evidence to suggest that adhering to the structure of a particular process in early meetings can give way to more open discussion as trust develops within the group. In the beginning, the structure of a particular process helps the group to focus its discussion on the student work rather than on the host of issues (schedules, availability of books or curriculum materials, the limited planning time available to teachers, and so on) that will inevitably arise in the course of the discussion. Through practice, groups incorporate into their discussions the principles behind the structured protocol, perhaps making the rigor of that structure less essential.

We needed the practice of going through the structured process. We couldn't have leaped to having this level of discussion [without it].

—High school department coordinator

The Process of Reflection. Reflection can occur through discussion and/or writing, preferably at the end of each meeting. Some processes (such as the Collaborative Assessment Conference and the Tuning Protocol) have built-in opportunities for reflection on both what was learned and on the process itself. Written reflections and notes from reflective discussions can provide important clues in planning future meetings.

> A high school teacher, after participating in a Tuning Protocol with teachers from many schools, reflected, "I didn't feel like we really had time to look at the student work. We need more time to really look through it, read one student's paper twice, maybe, before we can really say anything about it." This feedback was useful to teachers in planning future sessions.

You might want to draw on some of the following reflection questions to get you started:

- What did we learn?
- What worked well?
- Did the conversation move us closer to our goals? How?
- How did the discussion relate to other school issues?
- Did we do what we said we would—in terms of our purposes and our questions?
- Did we actually focus on students' work or on other issues?
- Did we follow the process as we planned? If not, why?
- How could the process be improved?
- How can we build on this to make examining student work a more frequent and important part of our own work?

What to Watch For. Are teachers learning about their students and their practice? Does the group leave with information, ideas, and agreement about what to do next?

Discussing student work sometimes brings out conflicting beliefs and assumptions about the kinds of work students should do; about how students' work should be assessed; about individual students' abilities and motivations; and about the ways teachers should teach. Is the facilitator aware of conflict as it arises? How do the facilitator and the group strive to maintain an honest, productive, and nonjudgmental discussion?

❖ CHAPTER 3 ❖

Crucial Considerations: Description, Interpretation, Evaluation, and Context

No two structures for looking at student work are quite the same. Some work for large groups, some for smaller groups. Some are designed to support looking at many samples of student work at once; some only one or two pieces. The list goes on. However, there are two aspects of design that deserve special attention. They are:

- *Mode of looking:* The degree to which the protocol encourages participants to "describe" or "interpret" or "evaluate" the work being presented.
- *The use of context:* The way and extent to which the protocol makes room for the presentation of the context of the work (background information about the student who created the work, the assignment, the conditions under which it was carried out, and so on).

In this chapter we will discuss each of these aspects and how they can shape the conversation depending on how they are used.

Description, Interpretation, or Evaluation?

How do description, interpretation, and evaluation differ? Consider these brief definitions and examples:

Description involves identifying in very literal terms what constitutes the piece of work being observed. Generally, there is little disagreement among group members about comments that are truly descriptive. Descriptive comments might sound like this:

- I see a yellow circle.
- I see that the yellow circle is surrounded by blue.
- There is no white space left on the page.

Interpretation involves assigning some meaning or intent to what is in the work. For example, the following comments involve interpretation (or speculation):

- There's a sun in a deep blue sky.
- I see a full moon in the night sky.
- That looks like a round, shiny UFO in outerspace.
- I think that the student was afraid of leaving any blank space on the page.

Evaluation attaches value or personal preference to the work being examined. For example:

- The sun is drawn skillfully.
- I see a very creative student at work here.
- I don't like the way there's no room left on the page—it feels so crowded.[1]

How Are These Different Modes of Looking Used with Student Work? Certainly, all of these kinds of comments have their places and value. However, many of the processes for looking at student work give particular emphasis to one or more of these kinds of comments and so require participants in that process to distinguish carefully among them. Some processes, such as the Collaborative Assessment Conference, give clear directions for participants to describe and then to interpret or speculate about what they see in the work. The Collaborative Assessment Conference never invites evaluation.

Other structures explicitly ask participants to make evaluative comments. For example, the Tuning Protocol invites "warm" and "cool" feedback. Depending on the focusing question, these judgments may be about the design of the exhibition or project, or about the student work itself. In fact, any process that involves measuring students' efforts against particular standards will require the participants to articulate some evaluations.

Making distinctions among these three kinds of comments is not always easy, even when a particular process gives specific directions to do so. Of these three types of responses, interpretations and evaluations come fairly easily for most. Description, however—specific, literal, careful description—often proves quite difficult. In "Learning from Looking," Steve Seidel offers the following thoughts about why:

---

1. Thanks to Steve Seidel for permission to elaborate on the examples he presented in "Learning from Looking" pp. 69–89 in N. Lyons, ed., *With Portfolio in Hand* (New York: Teachers College Press, 1998).

I suspect that two tendencies in our culture mix dangerously and make what should be a simple act of description far more difficult than one might anticipate. First, we tend to move very quickly and rarely stop to dwell at length on what is before our eyes. A trip to a museum to watch people looking at the art often confirms that most of us spend very little time looking at a single painting. Face to face with a Rembrandt, an extraordinary opportunity to observe the work of a master, to dwell on what many consider a major accomplishment of Western culture . . . most of us spend little more than a minute or two.

Further, we seem to be in the habit of making very quick judgments, even of things that might benefit from some reflection. We often expect of ourselves and our companions that we will know our thoughts, feelings, and opinions of a film before we've even crossed the street outside the theater. Exemplified by the film critics' Siskel and Ebert's "thumbs up" or "thumbs down," there is a "let's look at it once, declare it good or bad, and get on to the next" mentality that dominates our behavior perhaps a bit more than we might like to admit. (Seidel, 1998, p. 84)

To these general cultural tendencies are added the pressures and habits of the teaching profession. It is, in fact, part of an educator's responsibility to identify what students are doing well and what they're doing poorly, and to correct the wrongs quickly so that individual students don't fall too far behind in the curriculum that has to be covered. Circumstances often force everyone who works in education into the habit of making fast, almost automatic, evaluations when looking at students' work.

But many protocols for looking together at student work are designed to give teachers time. These protocols help everyone slow down, take a step back, and look calmly, carefully, and patiently in order to see what the student put into the work—before becoming involved in attaching personal interpretations and evaluations to it.

Why Are the Distinctions Important? In their first encounters with protocols that involve pure description, many teachers become frustrated with the apparent "triviality" of the conversation. And yet, with practice, there are many rewards that come from attending in such detail to the particular aspects of student work. Among those rewards are a renewed sensitivity to the complexity of students' thinking and more finely honed observational skills when looking at student work with and without the company of colleagues.

Focusing on description is not always the most appropriate way to accomplish the group's goals. However, given its often surprising benefits, you might want to consider experimenting with such a protocol (or developing one of your own) before relying wholly on ones that focus primarily on interpretation and evaluation.

Context

By "context" we mean all of the background information about the work being presented, the assignment that gave rise to it, and the student(s) who created it: What was the assignment? How was it graded? What criteria or rubrics were used? How much time were students given to work on it? What resources were available? Is this the kind of work the student usually does? Did the student seem to have difficulty with any part of it or seem to put a lot of effort into it? Did the student do this work at school or at home? Was help available at home? What did the student have to say about it while working on it and after it was completed? All of these concerns are part of the work's context.

How Is Presentation of Context Used in Looking at Student Work? Whether and how this context is presented to a group gathered to examine the work is a matter that varies according to the collaborative protocol being used. Some protocols call for the presenting teacher to describe the work's context at the beginning of the session as the work is introduced to the rest of the group. The Tuning Protocol is a good example of such a process: Immediately after the general introduction, the presenting teacher typically spends fifteen or twenty minutes telling the group about the assignment, goals, criteria, and other aspects of the context for the work before the group begins to examine it.

Other structures call for the context to be withheld initially. The group begins looking at the student work before any context is provided. In the Collaborative Assessment Conference, for example, the presenting teacher shows the group the piece of student work but tells them nothing about it. Only in the second half of the protocol, after the group has thoroughly examined, described, and asked questions about the work, does the presenting teacher tell them about the assignment, the grade level, who created the work, and how.

Why Is the Role of Context Important? When teachers first look at a piece of work, some of the first questions that spring to mind have to do with context. People naturally want to know about the assignment, the grade level, the background of the student, and so on. In a process that initially withholds that context, group members might feel frustrated at not being able to ask those questions. "Why should we guess about how old this student is or what he or she was trying to draw when the teacher can just tell us?" some people wonder.

The answer is straightforward: Not knowing the context forces participants to look at the work more closely—without preconceptions about what a student of a certain age ought to be able to do, or how a certain kind of prompt ought to be responded to. It also gives the presenting teacher the chance to hear fresh perspectives on students and their work. Often people who know neither the context nor the student will find in a piece of work evidence of important and powerful learning that presenting teachers miss because they are looking for something else or because they expect particular students to produce certain kinds of work.

Finally, withholding the context gives all the group's participants a chance to examine their own assumptions and preconceptions about how students carry out and convey meaning in their work. Many group members are surprised by one or several aspects of the context when it is revealed: The vivid artwork turns out to be the effort of a student whom they had never suspected of having artistic abilities; a student's reflection reveals that a research paper (which seemed to the group to involve a lot of effort and care) is in fact far less meaningful to the student than the service project that accompanied it. And so on.

As you consider choosing or designing a process for looking at student work, weigh carefully the role of context. The context you decide to share, and when you decide to share it, will have an impact on the kinds of issues and questions that arise. These subtle but powerful differences in approach and emphasis argue for careful, thoughtful, and repeated use of one protocol before moving on to others. As one district curriculum coordinator relates, "It takes three, four, five times with a protocol before the light goes on."

❖ CHAPTER 4 ❖

Two Ways of
Looking Together at
Student Work

In this chapter we describe two established structures for looking collaboratively at student work:

- The Tuning Protocol
- The Collaborative Assessment Conference

Figure 4.1 gives a quick overview of the key points of comparison and contrast between these two methods of looking at student work. A more detailed description of each process, along with bulleted agendas for each, follow.

You might use the following descriptions of the Tuning Protocol and the Collaborative Assessment Conference in several ways:

- If your group is in the early stages of deciding how to focus its efforts around student work, you might try out one or both of these processes in order to explore the opportunities and constraints of different formats.
- You might start with one of these models and alter or extend parts of it to suit better the goals of your particular group.
- You might use these processes as models for developing your own unique process.

A word of caution: If most members of the group are novices at looking collaboratively at student work, you might want to begin by choosing one or the other of these protocols and using it several times before modifying it or deciding to use a different process. These processes are tools and, as with any tool, they require practice in order for the user to gain the facility and comfort needed to derive the most benefit from them.

The Tuning Protocol: A Description

The Tuning Protocol was originally developed as a means for the five high schools in the Coalition of Essential Schools' Exhibitions Project to receive feedback from each other and fine-tune their developing student assessment systems, including exhibitions, portfolios, and design projects. Recognizing the complexities involved in developing new forms of assessment, the project staff, led by Joseph McDonald, developed a facilitated process to support teachers in sharing their students' work and their own work with colleagues, and reflecting on the lessons embedded there. Since its trial run in 1992, the Tuning Protocol has been widely used and adapted for professional development purposes in schools and among networks of teachers across the country.

To take part in the Tuning Protocol, teachers gather samples of their students' work on paper (and, whenever possible, on video), as well as some of the materials they have created to support student performance, such as written descriptions of the assignment and scoring rubrics. In a circle of about eight to twelve participants (usually other teachers), a facilitator leads the group through the process and keeps time. The presenting teacher, or team of teachers, describes the context for the student work (the task or project)—uninterrupted by questions or comments from participants.

Often the presenting teacher begins with a focusing question or area about which she would especially welcome feedback, for example, "Are you seeing evidence of persuasive writing in the student work?" Participants have time to examine the student work and ask clarifying questions. Then, with the presenting teacher listening but silent, participants offer "warm" and "cool" feedback. Warm feedback comes from a deliberately supportive, appreciative perspective; it points to what is strong in the work. Cool feedback comes from a deliberately challenging perspective; it questions what is missing or may need to be developed in the work. Presenting teachers benefit from the combination of warm and cool feedback.

Teachers often frame such feedback as questions, for example, "How might the project be different if students chose their own research topics?" After this feedback is offered, the presenting teacher has the opportunity, again uninterrupted, to reflect aloud on the feedback and address any of the comments or questions she chooses. Time is reserved for debriefing the experience.

A schedule for a Tuning Protocol appears in Figure 4.2. The schedule can be revised (times extended or condensed) to meet the needs of different groups of teachers and for different purposes.

Figure 4.1: Two Processes for Looking at Student Work

	Purposes	Role of Description, Interpretation, and/or Evaluation	Presentation of the Context for the Student Work	Kinds and Amount of Student Work Typically Shared
Tuning Protocol	To develop more effective exhibitions, projects, and assessment tasks. To develop common standards for students' work. To support teachers' instructional practice through focusing on student performances.	*Primarily evaluation:* The process asks participants to provide "warm" and "cool" feedback on student work samples and exhibition or project designs.	*Context presented initially:* At the beginning of the session, the presenting teachers typically provide descriptions (including documents) of the assignment, scoring criteria, as well as reflections from students and others.	*Kinds of pieces:* Most often used to look at work deriving from an exhibition or long-term project or portfolio. Sample work often includes brief video clip of student presentation as well as written and visual samples. *Number of pieces:* Typically used with work from several students. May also be used with a single sample.
Collaborative Assessment Conference	To learn more about students' goals: the problems and issues they choose to focus on in the course of an assignment. To learn more about the strengths and needs of a particular student. To reflect on and gather ideas for revising classroom practice.	*Primarily description, with some interpretation:* The process asks participants to describe the student work, to ask questions about it, and to speculate about the problem or issue in the work that the student was most focused on.	*Context withheld until middle of process:* The presenting teacher does not describe the context for the work until after participants have looked carefully at it and formulated questions about it.	*Kinds of pieces:* Most often used to look at student work drawn from student portfolios (e.g., a piece of art work or a sample of daily classwork). Works best with open-ended assignments (as opposed to worksheets). *Number of pieces:* Most often used to look at one or two pieces of work from a single student. May also be used with multiple samples.

Figure 4.2: Schedule for the Tuning Protocol
Developed by Joseph McDonald and David Allen

I. Introduction   10 min.

- Facilitator briefly introduces protocol goals, guidelines, and schedule.
- Participants briefly introduce themselves.

II. Teacher presentation   20 min.

- Teacher-presenter describes the context for student work (assignment, scoring rubric, etc.).
- Teacher-presenter poses her focusing question for feedback.
- Participants are silent.

III. Clarifying questions   5 min. max

- Participants ask clarifying questions.
- Facilitator judges which questions more properly belong in warm/cool feedback (i.e., questions that involve more than a very brief, factual answer).

IV. Examination of student work samples   15 min.

- Samples of student work might be original or photocopied pieces of written work and/or video clips of presentations.

V. Pause to reflect on warm and cool feedback   2–3 min. max.

- Participants may take a couple of minutes to reflect silently on what they would like to contribute to the feedback session.

VI. Warm and cool feedback   15 min.

- Participants share feedback while teacher-presenter is silent.
- Facilitator may remind participants of teacher-presenter's focusing question (Step II).

VII. Reflection   15 min.

- Teacher-presenter speaks to those comments/questions he or she chooses to.
- Facilitator may intervene to focus, clarify, etc.
- Participants are silent.

VIII. Debrief   10 min.

- Facilitator leads an open discussion of the tuning experience the group has shared: What was effective? What concerns did the process raise?

Guidelines for Tuning Protocol. Participation in a structured process of professional collaboration like this can be intimidating and anxiety producing, especially for the teacher presenting student work. Having a shared set of guidelines, or norms, helps everybody participate in a manner that is respectful as well as conducive to helpful feedback. Below is one set of guidelines; your group may want to create its own. In any case, the group should go over the guidelines and the schedule before starting the protocol. The facilitator must feel free to remind participants of the guidelines and schedule at any time in the process.

- *Be respectful of teacher-presenter(s).* By making their work more public, teachers are exposing themselves to kinds of critiques they may not be used to. Participants need to be thoughtful about how they phrase comments or questions. Inappropriate comments or questions should be reworded or withdrawn.
- *Contribute to substantive discussion.* Many teachers may be accustomed to blanket praise. Without thoughtful, probing "cool" questions and comments, they won't benefit from the Tuning Protocol.
- *Be respectful of the facilitator's role, particularly in regard to following the guidelines and keeping time.* A Tuning Protocol that doesn't allow for all parts will do a disservice to the teacher-presenters and to the participants.

The Tuning Protocol in Action. Two high schools in neighboring districts on Long Island had been developing schoolwide goals for student performance. The principals considered how the two schools could become "critical friends" in helping each other address their goals. In conversation with members of their faculties and a researcher from Annenberg Institute, they decided to use the Tuning Protocol as a way to help each of the schools connect its goals to classroom practice and student learning.

While the student performance goals for the schools varied somewhat, the principals were able to identify a small number of complementary goals on which to focus, including improving student writing across genres; improving oral communications skills; and developing and supporting an informed opinion. Each of the schools selected a group of 10–12 teachers from the science, math, and English departments to meet regularly to present and get feedback on projects and student work samples that reflect the goals.

The teachers met for a full day four times during the year, alternating between the two schools. In small-group discussions by discipline, a teacher (or team of teachers) presented a project and framed a focusing question that related to the school-wide goal. Following the structure of the Tuning Protocol, the group asked clarifying questions, examined student work samples, and provided "warm" and "cool" feedback. Typically, each group went through two Tuning Protocols during the day with one presentation from each school.

In one meeting, a veteran science teacher presented his students' research projects. One of his school's goals for student performance was "Developing and supporting an informed opinion." He began with the focusing question: "How can a rubric that includes presentation skills be used as a teaching tool as well as an assessment instrument?" Participants viewed a video of a student presenting his research on conductivity and looked at the written outline for the presentation. In giving feedback, the teachers considered how students would benefit from viewing videotapes of prior presentations and discussing—even using—the rubric before they presented.

In his reflection, the presenting teacher recognized the value of the group's feedback. "The protocol will have an immediate impact in my practice." Reflecting on comments from the protocol, he talked about showing students videotapes of prior performances and asking students to evaluate them and to discuss them using the rubric. "The rubric itself is not the teaching tool, it's a discussion tool." He also commented on the value of the Tuning Protocol structure: "I wouldn't have been able to hold back if not for the training of the Tuning Protocol, and so I wouldn't have heard the kinds of feedback I did."

The Tuning Protocol provided the structure for the conversation and helped keep the focus on student learning. After three sessions, teachers felt a level of trust within the group and recognized that their conversations had begun to address core questions of teaching and learning, such as how goals for student performance can be brought to life in the projects students do and assessed in the work they produce.

The Collaborative Assessment Conference: A Description

Since its development by Steve Seidel and colleagues at Harvard Project Zero in 1988, the Collaborative Assessment Conference has been used for a variety of purposes: to hone teachers' ability to look closely at and to interpret students' work; to explore the strengths and needs of a particular child; to reflect on the work collected in student portfolios; and to foster conversations among faculty about the work students are doing and how to support that work. It provides a structure for teachers to look together at a piece of work, first to determine what it reveals about the student and the issues that student cares about, and then to consider the implications of that student's issues and concerns for teaching and learning in general. The structure for the conference evolved from three key ideas:

- First, students use school assignments, especially open-ended ones, to tackle important problems in which they are personally interested. Sometimes these problems are the same ones that the teacher has assigned them to work on, sometimes not. This means that a piece of student work has the potential to reveal not only the student's mastery of class goals, but also a wealth of information about the student, including his or her intellectual interests, strengths, and struggles.
- Second, adults can only begin to see and understand the serious work that students undertake if they suspend judgment long enough to look carefully and closely at what is actually in the work, rather than what they hope or expect to see in it.
- Third, teachers need the perspectives of others (especially those who are not familiar with their students or classroom contexts) to help reveal the many facets of a student's work and to help generate ideas about how to use this information to shape daily practice.

In Collaborative Assessment Conferences, the presenting teacher brings a piece of student work to share with a group of five to ten colleagues (usually other teachers and administrators). The process begins with the presenting teacher showing (or distributing copies of) the piece to the group. Throughout the first part of the conference, the presenting teacher says nothing—giving no information about the student, the assignment, or the context in which the student worked.

Through a series of questions asked by the facilitator (such as, "What do you see in the work?"), the group works to understand the piece by describing it in detail, raising questions about it, and speculating about the problems or issues with which the student was most engaged. They do this without making evaluations about the quality of the work or its appeal to their personal tastes. The facilitator helps this process by asking participants to point out the evidence in the work on which they based the judgments that inevitably slip out. (For example, if someone comments that the work seems very creative, the facilitator might ask the participant to describe the aspect of the work that led him or her to say that.)

In the second part of the conference, the focus broadens. Having concentrated intensively on the piece itself, the group, in conversation with the presenting teacher, now considers the conditions under which the work was created as well as broader issues of teaching and learning. First, the presenting teacher provides any information that she thinks is relevant about the context for the work. This might include describing the assignment, responding to the discussion, answering questions raised in the first part of the conference (though the presenting teacher can choose which of those questions to respond to), describing other work by the child, and/or commenting on how her own reading or observation of the work compares to that of the group's.

Next, the facilitator asks the whole group (presenting teacher included) to reflect on the ideas generated by the discussion of the piece. These might be reflections about specific next steps for the child in question, or ideas about what the participants might do in their own classes, or thoughts about the teaching and learning process in general. Finally, the whole group reflects on the conference itself.

Figure 4.3 is a working agenda for a Collaborative Assessment Conference. The time allotted for each step of the conference is not fixed, since the time needed for each step will vary according to the work being considered. At each stage, the facilitator makes the decision about when to move the group on to the next step. Typically, Collaborative Assessment Conferences take from 45 minutes to an hour and 15 minutes.

Figure 4.3: Steps in the Collaborative Assessment Conference Developed by Steve Seidel and Project Zero Colleagues

I. Getting started

- The group chooses a facilitator who will make sure the group stays focused on the particular issue addressed in each step.
- The presenting teacher puts the selected work in a place where everyone can see it or provides copies for the other participants. She says nothing about the work, the context in which it was created, or the student until Step V.
- The participants observe or read the work in silence, perhaps making brief notes about aspects of it that they particularly notice.

II. Describing the work

- The facilitator asks the group, "What do you see?"
- Group members respond without making interpretations, evaluations about the quality of the work, or statements of personal preference.
- If evaluations or interpretations emerge, the facilitator asks the person to describe the evidence on which those comments are based.

(continued)

Figure 4.3 *(Continued)*

III. Asking questions about the work

- The facilitator asks the group, "What questions does this work raise for you?"
- Group members state any questions they have about the work, the child, the assignment, the circumstances under which the work was carried out, and so on.
- The presenting teacher makes notes about these question (but does not answer them).

IV. Speculating about what the student is working on

- The facilitator asks the group, "What do you think the child is working on?"
- Participants, drawing on their observation of the work, make suggestions about the problems or issues that the student focused on in carrying out the assignment.

V. Hearing from the presenting teacher

- The facilitator invites the presenting teacher to speak.
- The presenting teacher provides her perspective on the student's work, describing what she sees in it and adding any other information that she feels is important to share with the group. She may choose respond to some or all of the questions raised by the group in Step 3.
- The presenting teacher also comments on anything surprising or unexpected that she heard during the describing, questioning, and speculating phases.

VI. Discussing implications for teaching and learning

- The facilitator invites all participants, including the presenting teacher, to share any thoughts they have about their own teaching, students' learning, or ways to support this particular student in future instruction.

VII. Reflecting on the collaborative assessment conference

- The group reflects together on their experiences of or reactions to the conference as a whole or to particular parts of it.

VIII. Thanking the presenting teacher.

- The session concludes with acknowledgment of and thanks to the presenting teacher.

The Collaborative Assessment Conference in Action. At an urban middle school in Massachusetts, teachers felt that they needed to "do more" with what students put into their folders. "I give the students time to reflect on their work, but I don't ever have time to reflect on it," said one teacher, to a chorus of head-nodding from others on the faculty. The school decided to institute regular Collaborative Assessment Conferences in order to give teachers more time to reflect on and discuss their students' work.

The school designated one of the weekly planning sessions each month to carrying out a Collaborative Assessment Conference. The teachers took turns bringing a piece (or pieces) of work from one of their students. To lead the meetings, the principal invited facilitators from outside the school who were well versed in the Collaborative Assessment Conference.

At first, the protocol felt awkward. Many teachers were uncomfortable with having to describe and ask questions about a piece of work without knowing the assignment or the context in which the student was working. "It would be a lot easier if we knew more about the assignment and the student," several teachers commented as they reflected on the session.

The presenting teachers were the first to identify the power of excluding context in the initial discussion. One commented, "When people began asking questions about the work, like 'What did this student learn the most about while putting together this project?', I realize just how much I don't know about my students." She continued, "It gives me ideas for what I need to go back and talk with them about." Another teacher realized that he never would have noticed the amount of effort and detail that went into a drawing that accompanied an essay without the benefit of other teachers' comments: "I was more focused on the writing part of the assignment. But as the other teachers described it, I started to see that the student had captured an important theme in that picture."

Over time, as the teachers became more comfortable with the Collaborative Assessment Conference, they found that the process helped them to identify important school-wide concerns: how to balance supporting students in long-term projects with encouraging them to work independently; how to tie important curriculum topics to student interests; how to get clearer with students about the standards and criteria for their work. These issues became topics for whole school faculty meetings. One teacher summed up the importance of arriving at these issues through looking at student work:

> It's not like we couldn't have decided to concentrate on one of these issues without having gone through the Collaborative Assessment Conference. But,

somehow, letting those issues grow out of looking at student work makes them feel more real, more grounded, more important. It's not someone telling us to pay attention to a particular issue. It's that we see the need for it ourselves in our students' work.

❖ CHAPTER 5 ❖

Two Schools That Developed Their Own Processes

Existing strategies for looking at student work abound. Yet, chances are good that, in order to achieve your and your school's particular goals, you may need to adapt those existing strategies or develop new ones. This chapter contains examples of two schools doing exactly that. With specific goals in mind, the two faculties set out to shape their own processes for examining and discussing student work. Their stories offer examples of processes that were developed in response to specific needs and for specific contexts (in contrast to the models in Chapter 4, which were designed for general use). Each example is presented in five parts, mirroring the steps described in Chapter 2:

1. Taking stock of current ways of looking at student work
2. Establishing goals and framing questions
3. Developing a process for looking collaboratively at student work
4. Implementing the process
5. Reflecting on and revising the process

Bringing Outsiders In: Using Student Work to Train Exhibition Judges

In the spring of 1995, the Exhibition Committee at Rosemont Middle School faced a knotty problem. As with the other two ATLAS schools[1] in

---

1. The ATLAS Communities project began as a collaboration among four organizations (the Coalition of Essential Schools at Brown University; Education Development Center, in Newton, MA; Project Zero at Harvard University; and the School Development Program at Yale University) and three school systems (Gorham, ME; Norfolk, VA; and Prince George's County, MD). The goal of the initial collaboration was to develop a comprehensive approach to school reform. The ATLAS Communities project continues to work with school districts, using its approach to help schools examine their management structures, curricula, instructional approaches, and assessment practices. For more information, contact ATLAS Commmunities, 55 Chapel St., Newton, MA 02158-1060 (http://www.edc.org/FSC/ATLAS).

Norfolk, Virginia, the faculty of Rosemont had committed itself to holding public student exhibitions with "outside" judges—people from outside the school who would sit on panels with Rosemont teachers to assess the students' presentations. Rosemont's Exhibition Committee (composed of several faculty members and an administrator) anticipated that there would be many concerns about this plan—from teachers, parents, students, and the prospective judges themselves. The committee's main concern, however, was helping community members who would be serving as judges to carry out their roles in a way that would ensure the best possible learning experience for all the students.

Taking Stock. Student exhibitions (research papers and oral presentations) had been instituted the previous year and had proven to be a daunting challenge for both the students and the faculty. Even though the faculty had been reshaping the curriculum to include more performance-oriented and hands-on activities, the students still struggled with the unfamiliar tasks of researching and managing long-term projects. A new and time-consuming mentoring system (whereby groups of two to six students were paired with each teacher, staff member, and administrator in the school) presented stubborn organizational problems that the entire staff wrestled with over the course of the year.

Ultimately, in order to keep students from being penalized by the inevitable glitches in the new system, the school decided against having students present their exhibitions to a public panel at the end of that first year. Rather, teachers at all grade levels were encouraged to help their students to carry out projects related to the topics and issues already studied in the curriculum. Twenty students were asked to present their work to an audience of students, parents, teachers, and other adults. Although the audience members were allowed to ask questions of the student presenters, no formal assessment of their work was made, since the classroom teachers had already assigned the students grades for their work.

At the beginning of the second year of exhibitions, however, the faculty felt ready to take the next step: turning the public exhibitions into occasions for assessment and evaluation. Everyone agreed that this aspect of the exhibition presentation was important. But the idea of inviting outsiders in to play such a critical role raised several concerns for Rosemont's staff.

Some were troubled by the prospect of exposing students' work to the scrutiny of people who might not understand what to expect of middle school students. "If the outside judges don't know our students or where they started or what we teach or how we teach it, how can they judge the work fairly?" wondered one teacher. An administrator pointed out that the process was likely to be as uncomfortable for teachers as for students, since looking at the students' work was like "holding up a mirror" to the teachers' work. Given that teaching had until recent years been a solitary undertaking at the school, and given that the whole process of supporting exhibitions in the classrooms was still new, people were not sure what to expect by inviting virtual strangers to peer more closely into that mirror.

Jane Montagna, a member of the Rosemont's Exhibition Committee and the staff developer for the school, had another worry. Earlier in the year, she, along with members of the exhibition committees of all three ATLAS Schools in Norfolk, had participated in a modified Tuning Protocol session facilitated by ATLAS staff members who were visiting the schools. In that session, they had looked at videotapes of student exhibitions and discussed the quality of the students' work.

After that session, Jane had conducted similar meetings for Rosemont's teachers. The meetings focused on reviewing samples from the previous year's student exhibitions. The goal as she saw it was to help teachers think about the purposes of exhibitions and how to help students build the skills necessary to carry them out. From discussions in these meetings, she had discovered a sharp divide: Some believed that the most important aspect of an exhibition at this level was the degree to which it supported students' self-esteem. Others thought that the primary purpose of the exhibition was to push students to think more deeply about the issue that they had studied. She realized that this was bound to be a critical issue for all who would be serving as judges for the exhibitions—the people from outside the school as well as the teachers.

Establishing Goals and Framing Questions. To address these worries and to ensure that the exhibition process would be a good one for both the students and the panel judges, the Exhibition Committee knew that some initial training with the prospective judges was needed. With Jane taking the lead, the Exhibition Committee settled on two goals for the training session:

- To help judges develop an appreciation of Rosemont's goals for student exhibitions as a vehicle for deepening students' understanding of a topic.
- To raise the judges' awareness about the role of personal experience and bias in exhibition judging.

Jane explained the first goal:

It's not just about asking the easy questions that make the kids feel good because they can give an answer. And it's not just about who can give the smoothest presentation. We really want people to question the kids in a way that gets at the kids' understanding.

The second goal grew out of the committee's recognition that people see the judge's role in very different ways. While the members of the committee did not want to suggest that one definition of the judge's role was the "right" one, they did want to give the judges the opportunity to think about, clarify, and compare with others their own understanding of the role of judge and how their personal experiences might affect their judgments.

Developing a Process. It didn't take long for the committee to decide that the best way to prepare people for looking at student work was to spend the training session looking at and discussing student exhibitions similar to the ones the "trainees" would encounter as judges. In consultation with the Exhibition Committee, the staff developers at the other ATLAS Schools, and the researchers from the ATLAS Project, Jane designed the core of the "Judges Training Session": having the participants watch videos of two brief student exhibitions and then address some questions about each. The questions were aimed at getting people to think in concrete ways about the two goals for the session. The agenda was as follows:

Agenda for Judges Training

1. Welcome and presentation of goals
2. Small group discussions in which each person in the group answers the question, "What is the role of a judge?" [Group spokesperson reports the small group's discussion to the large group]
3. Viewing of first videotape of a student exhibition [The tape is stopped just before the judges on the tape begin asking questions of the student]
4. Whole-group discussion of the question: "If you were the judge, what questions would you ask this student?" [Group discusses the question, then watches the actual questioning session on tape and compares their questions]
5. Viewing of second videotape of a student exhibition
6. Whole group discussion of the questions: "How did you feel as you watched the tape? What do you think the judges did well (or not)?"
7. Brief description of developmental issues of middle school children
8. Questions and concerns

Implementing the Process. On the day of the training, 20 prospective judges assembled in the middle school's library to reflect on the purposes of exhibitions and the role of judge. The group consisted of administrators from the district office, staff from the district attorney's office (including the district attorney), parents, high school teachers, high school students, and a few middle school teachers. Jane introduced the goals and the agenda for the training and then led the group through the various activities.

In the initial discussion of the role of judge, most members of the group gave similar responses. However, differences in points of view began to emerge as the group discussed the specific student exhibitions they had watched on the videotape, especially after they had watched the second one. The first video clip had depicted a confident and well-prepared student who gave her presentation smoothly and responded to her judges' questions quickly and thoughtfully. In the second video clip, however, the presenting student appeared to struggle more. Her presentation, which she appeared to have memorized, was recited softly, almost mechanically. When the videotape showed the judges asking her questions, the student was often silent for a period, furrowing her brow and twisting her hands behind her as she tried to think of answers. Her answers were often halting.

Jane asked the group, "What were your thoughts as you watched the second exhibition?" One participant responded, "I thought the judges' questions created too many negative experiences for that child. They kept asking questions at a higher level, instead of easing up when they saw she couldn't handle it. I felt terrible watching it. I felt like I wanted to get out of there for her." "I had those feelings, too," responded another participant, "but if we don't have some questions of a probing nature, we're negating the whole purpose of what the students are doing. And we need to allow them time to think."

Another participant returned to the issue of how to make the presenter comfortable: "The judges [on the videotape] should have started with a less challenging question when they saw how nervous she was." A fourth participant pointed out that, in fact, no more than 12 seconds elapsed between the time a question was asked and the time she answered. ("I started timing when I saw how much time she was taking," he explained.) "And she always came up with an answer," another offered, "It just took her longer than we were comfortable with."

The debate was not resolved in favor of one questioning approach or another, but the participants' reflections at the end of the session revealed that collaboratively examining the student's work had given them some valuable strategies to carry with them to their own panels. "I realized the importance of the nonverbal communication. It's important to be able to read body language in order to help the student do her best. If a student looks really uncomfortable, I want to be sure to give her a little more support, like an encouraging nod or a smile."

One participant commented that the question period seemed to reveal much more about what the student understood than the presentation did: "Obviously, [the student in the video] knew much more than she stated in her presentation. Only the questions got that knowledge out of her." Another agreed: "I want to be very careful about how I ask questions—it's hard to walk that line between making the child feel comfortable so she can do her best and finding out what she really knows."

Reflecting on the Process. The next day the public exhibitions began. Over the course of the week, both the strengths and the weaknesses of the training session emerged. The experience of looking at student exhibitions on videotape proved valuable: "It was extremely helpful to see what an exhibition looked like before I had to judge one—even seeing one in which the judges were not very good. At least it told me what I didn't want to do." Another commented, "I'm glad I got to hear what other people thought about the same presentation. It made me realize that there's no right way to be a judge."

Judges, as well as teachers not involved in the judging process, voiced concern over the lack of common standards for assessing the students' work. While everyone felt prepared for the question-and-answer period, they had not had time to practice actually scoring presentations and papers. Several mentioned that more practice scoring student work and comparing results might have helped with this issue. Others pointed out that clearer criteria would have helped.

A final concern emerged about panels on which all the judges adopted the same approach to the role, so that all were either wholehearted supporters or critical questioners, creating an unchallenging experience for students in the first case and a too-challenging one for them in the second. Jane reflected that, given a little more time, the training session might have enabled her to size up the preferred approaches of individual judges and to create more balanced panels—panels that included both judges who "pushed" and judges who "comforted." "Good ideas for next year," Jane pointed out.

Parent-Student-Teacher Conferences:
Looking at Student Work from Multiple Perspectives

The faculty of the Charles Shaw Middle School in Gorham, Maine, wanted to fine-tune its assessment processes. They wanted students to take more responsibility for their learning. They also wanted to allow for more individualized attention, for more parent participation, and for a continuing focus on looking at and discussing the things that students do and make.

Taking Stock. Alternative assessment strategies had long been part of the Gorham, Maine, School District's approach to education when it became a member of the ATLAS Communities project in 1993. Students in every school in the district kept portfolios, gave periodic "benchmark exhibitions," and carried out mandatory written and oral performances assessed with criteria common to all the schools. In addition, years before when the staff had initiated portfolio work, they had begun using Collaborative Assessment Conferences as a way to help teachers talk together about student work. (See Chapter 4 for a description of the Collaborative Assessment Conference.)

Teachers and administrators, though, were not entirely satisfied with the assessment process. At Shaw Middle School, teachers and administrators tried to pinpoint this dissatisfaction in reflections at staff meetings. Eventually, they identified three problems with their current methods of assessing student work:

- Open houses and parent conferences, which mainly focused on report cards, did not provide parents with an in-depth opportunity for learning about student goals and performances.
- Students did not have specific personal goals for which they felt accountable. Nor did they understand the standards or criteria by which their work was being evaluated.
- Forging alliances with parents to foster the education of their children was difficult when parents did not understand the goals for their children and had no chance to examine their children's work in order to see how the children were achieving those goals.

Establishing Goals and Framing Questions. Based on these concerns, the Shaw staff articulated the specific goals that they wanted to achieve with a new process of looking at student work:

- To increase communication among parents, teachers, and students
- To delineate the different responsibilities of parents, teachers, and student in the student's education
- To link student performances to specific individualized and personal goals for each student, and to use those performances to gauge how well the goals were being met
- To discuss meaningful interventions to foster continued growth and development for each student

Developing a Process. Shaw Middle School's School Planning and Management Team, an advisory body composed of teachers, administrators, parents, community members, and students, began to explore ways of making the assessment process more meaningful for students and teachers. Drawing on the teachers' experiences with the Collaborative Assessment Conference, the School Planning and Management Team began considering the possibility of developing a Parent-Student-Teacher conference that would enable parents, their children, and teachers to look at and discuss the children's work on a regular basis.

In 1994, after much debate, the members of the School Planning and Management Team decided to include students in the traditional Parent-Teacher conferences. They also decided that the major activity of those conferences would be looking at and discussing pieces of student work and that the students themselves would take the major responsibility for organizing and running the conference. The School Planning and Management Team presented the idea to the Shaw faculty, which worked out the details of implementation. (A year later, the district endorsed the idea of Parent-Student-Teacher conferences and set aside time for such conferences in all schools at designated points throughout the school year, extending the school calendar to create time for the conferences and adding staff development to help teachers prepare for them.)

The original implementation plan developed by the faculty involved holding conferences twice a year. Three days in September and three days in March were devoted to half-hour-long conferences with each student and her or his parents or guardians. Both conferences centered on examining and discussing the work that the student presented. In the September conference (known as the "entry conference"), teachers, parents, and students reviewed work in order to help the students set personal goals for their learning for the year. The later conference gave everyone a chance to examine students' work for evidence of progress toward those goals.

Implementing the Process. Recognizing that this approach differed significantly from what parents and students were used to, the faculty at Shaw took steps to prepare themselves, as well as students and parents, for the conferences. Before the start of school in the fall, teachers participated in staff development activities that helped them explore ways of setting individual student goals with students and parents. They also considered various formats for the "entry conference" meeting in September. During these sessions, they worked in small groups and, using actual pieces of student work, role-played different scenarios. They practiced explaining the rationale for such conferences to students and parents, and, in the process, discussed many of their own concerns and reservations about the new approach.

During the initial weeks of school, teachers and students considered various ways of documenting the students' work and progress. The teachers reminded students that their portfolios were not collections of "best works," but rather places where they could gather pieces of work that showed their growth in knowledge or skills. Initial drafts, revisions, completed works, and their own reflections on their work could all provide evidence of that growth.

Teachers also discussed with students the process of goal-setting: They explained the rationale for the process, distinguished between long- and short-range goals, discussed obstacles to reaching them, and emphasized the need for periodic "check-ins" to monitor and assess progress. Some teachers asked students to discuss their preliminary goals at home with their parents so that the first conference could focus on refining the goals and discussing how to reach them.

Before the first conference, teachers sent a letter home to parents explaining the aims and organization of the Parent-Student-Teacher conference. Some teachers included with the letter a list of questions that the parents and students could discuss together before the conference ("When do I learn best?", "What do I want my teacher to know about me?").

The students took responsibility for establishing the focus of the Parent-Student-Teacher conference. They selected one or two pieces of their work to present at the conference, pieces which they felt represented both some of their strengths and the areas in which they wanted to improve. After considering the work, student, parent, and teacher concentrated on articulating goals and developing action plans that would help the student to work toward them, both at school and at home. The conversations were led by students, with the teachers serving as facilitators. As one teacher explained:

> A major student goal might be, "I want to get better organized." My challenge is to become a good facilitator and ask, "Laurie, what do you mean by that? How will we know if you are better organized when we get together again? What can you do to prove that you are better organized?"

Reflecting on the Process. Drawing on their strong tradition of reflective practice, the Shaw teachers stopped to ponder what they were learning at every step of the way during the Parent-Student-Teacher conference. They wrote personal reflections during staff development meetings; they discussed their preparation for the conferences as well as the conferences themselves during regular team meetings; they sent out questionnaires to parents and analyzed and distributed the results. Through these reflections, the faculty was able to identify many strengths in the Parent-Student-

Teacher conferences as they had been designed:

- *Preconference organization and preparation:* The faculty felt that their attention to this area had been energy well spent. As one teacher pointed out, "People really need support whenever they try something new, and particularly when the extended community is invited to become actively involved."

- *Focus on actual pieces of student work and their connection to specific goals:* The faculty agreed that their initial focus on the connection between goals and student performances was important and should continue to be emphasized. Many also cited the importance of having the actual work at the center of the conversation. One teacher explained, "With the portfolio on the table, it was easy to convey to parents the reason for poor performances—a reason based not on ability but on certain choices made by the student."

- *Student involvement:* Most of the faculty were pleased with the active role students played in the Parent-Student-Teacher conference. Parents showed great pride as they watched their children assume ownership of their work and participate in the conversations. In addition, many teachers felt the "burden of proof" shift from their shoulders to the students':

  > The Parent-Student-Teacher conference was the easiest conference I've ever had. It was not incumbent on me to take responsibility for defining the progress the student had made. I was an observer in the process that involved meaningful conversation focused on student work. The onus was on the child to talk about her own work intelligently and confidently, to describe what she had learned and how she would use that learning in the future.

- *Parent involvement:* After the initial conference, the staff at Shaw polled parents on the effectiveness of various aspects of the conference. More than 70% of the parents who responded to the poll rated as "very helpful" (the highest rating) the conference's focus on their child as a learner; the process of setting goals with their child and the child's teacher; and their child's participation in the conference. For the teachers, the Parent-Student-Teacher conferences become another way to invite parents to support the education of their children.

- *Administrative support:* Many teachers acknowledged the central role that the administration had played in nurturing the success of the first round of Parent-Student-Teacher conferences. With such encouragement, teachers felt free to take the risks required to launch a new assessment process. As one teacher noted, "It's critical to have a supportive administration that recognizes this process will not be flawless."

The faculty's reflection process also generated several points for improvement in future Parent-Student-Teacher conferences. First, they expanded the time allotted for the August in-service professional development dedicated to preparing for the conferences. The extra time allowed them to address in more depth the key elements of the initial Parent-Student-Teacher conference and the things each conference participant needs to do in order to prepare for it.

Second, they realized that September was too early in the year for students to formulate goals. They proposed that at the end of the year, students select several pieces of work from their portfolios to carry with them to next year's class. Then, when students were asked to draft goals at the beginning of the year, they would have a more substantive body of work to refer to. The teachers also recommended to the district that the six conference days be reallocated. Instead of three entry conference days in the fall and three final conference days in the spring, they proposed three periods of two days each, thus providing a mid-year "check-in" conference.

Finally, the teachers suggested several steps to further encourage both parents and students to take active roles in the learning and assessment processes:

- Invite parents to a forum in the fall to explain the rationale for the Parent-Student-Teacher conference.
- Make sure the letter sent ahead to parents passes the "kitchen table test" (i.e., that it is clear and free of education jargon).
- Create more opportunities (in addition to the Parent-Student-Teacher conference) for students to share and celebrate their work.

While all agreed that bringing parents, students, and teachers together to look at student work took a degree of organization, energy, and time not required by the more traditional conferences, many teachers also acknowledged the added meaning and value it had brought to the assessment process. One teacher summed it up:

Good teachers have always looked thoughtfully at student work. We've used formative and summative evaluations and in-class conferencing. We've always looked at student work and hoped we would target improvement in the next learning experience. With the Parent-Student-Teacher conference, we've taken that process to a new, collaborative level. We've come to recognize what little value there is in just slapping an A or a D on student work. Goals emerge through the process of reflection on and discussion of that work. Assessment is no longer an isolated, one-shot deal.

As these two case studies demonstrate, teachers and administrators are taking the lead in using and developing protocols that help them reflect on the work that students do. Looking together at student work provides guideposts for more effective teaching.

❖ APPENDIX ❖

Resources Related to Looking at Student Work

About Looking at Student Work (General)

Allen, D. (Ed.). (1998). *Assessing student learning: From grading to understanding.* New York: Teachers College Press.

Annenberg Institute for School Reform. (1997). *Looking at student work: A window into the classroom* [Video]. New York: Teachers College Press.

Cushman, K. (1996). Looking collaboratively at student work: An essential toolkit [whole issue]. *Horace, 13*(2). [Available from the Coalition of Essential Schools*]

Hatch, T., & Seidel, S. (1997). Putting student work on the table. *National Forum, 77* (1), 18–21.

About the Collaborative Assessment Conference

Seidel, S. (1998). Learning from looking. In N. Lyons (Ed.), *With portfolio in hand: Validating the new teacher professionalism* (pp. 69–89). New York: Teachers College Press.

Seidel, S., Walters, J., Kirby, E., Olff, N., Powell, K., Scripp, L., & Veenema, S. (1996). *Portfolio practices: Thinking through the assessment of student work.* Washington, DC: NEA Publications Library. [Available from Harvard Project Zero*]

Seidel, S. (1998). Wondering to be done: The collaborative assessment conference. In D. Allen (Ed.), *Assessing student learning: From grading to understanding* (pp. 21–39). New York: Teachers College Press.

About the Tuning Protocol

Allen, D. (1995). *The Tuning Protocol: A process for reflection.* Providence, RI: Coalition of Essential Schools. [Available from the Coalition of Essential Schools*]

---

* Indicates that the address for obtaining the work is included at the end of this list under "Organizations"

Allen, D. (1998). The Tuning Protocol: Opening up reflection. In D. Allen (Ed.), *Assessing student learning: From grading to understanding* (pp. 87–104). New York: Teachers College Press.

McDonald, J. P. (1996). *Redesigning school: Lessons for the 21st century.* San Francisco: Jossey-Bass.

McDonald, J. P., Smith, S., Turner, D., Finney, M., & Barton, E. (1993). *Graduation by exhibition: Assessing genuine achievement.* Arlington, VA: Association for Supervision and Curriculum Development.

About Descriptive Review Processes

Andrias, J., Kanevsky, R. D., Strieb, L. Y., & Traugh, C. (1992). *Exploring values and standards: Implications for assessment.* New York: Columbia University/ NCREST. [Available from NCREST*]

Carini, P. (1982). *The school lives of seven children: A five-year study.* Grand Forks: University of North Dakota/North Dakota Study Group on Evaluation. [Available from the North Dakota Study Group*]

Cochran-Smith, M., & Lytle, S. (1993). *Inside/outside: Teacher research and knowledge.* New York: Teachers College Press. [See Chapter 7: "Oral Inquiries" for information on the Descriptive Review of a Child.]

Featherstone, H. (1998). Studying children: The Philadelphia Teachers' Learning Cooperative. In D. Allen (Ed.), *Assessing student learning: From grading to understanding* (pp. 66–83). New York: Teachers College Press.

Kanevsky, R. D. (1993). The descriptive review of a child. In L. Darling-Hammond, L. Einbender, F. Frelow, & J. Ley-King (Eds.), *Authentic assessment in practice: A collection of portfolios, performance tasks, exhibitions, and documentation.* New York: Columbia University/NCREST [Available from NCREST*]

Snyder, J., Lieberman, A., Macdonald, M. B., & Goodwin, A. L. (1992). *Makers of meaning in a learning-centered school: A case study of Central Park East 1 Elementary School.* New York: Columbia University/NCREST. [Available from NCREST*]

About the Primary Language Record

Barrs, M., Ellis, S., Hester, H., & Thomas, A. (1989). *The Primary Language Record: Handbook for teachers.* Portsmouth, NH: Heinemann.

Falk, B. (1998). Looking at students and their work: Supporting diverse learners with the Primary Language Record. In D. Allen (Ed.), *Assessing student learning: From grading to understanding.* (pp. 40–65). New York: Teachers College Press.

Falk, B., & Darling-Hammond, L. (1993). *The Primary Language Record at P.S. 261: How assessment transforms teaching and learning.* New York: Columbia University/NCREST. [Available from NCREST*]

Falk, B., MacMurdy, S., & Darling-Hammond, L. (1995). *Taking a different look: How the Primary Language Record supports teaching for diverse learners.* New York: Columbia University/NCREST. [Available from NCREST*]

About Exhibitions

Central Park East Secondary School. (1995) *Graduation by portfolio* [Video]. [Available from Central Park East Secondary School, 1573 Madison Ave., New York, NY 10029]

Coalition of Essential Schools. (1994). *Dimensions of an exhibition* [Video]. [Available from the Coalition of Essential Schools*]

McDonald, J. P. (1991). *Exhibitions: Facing outward, pointing inward.* Providence, RI: Coalition of Essential Schools. [Available from the Coalition of Essential Schools*]

McDonald, J. P., Smith, S., Turner, D., Finney, M., & Barton, E. (1993). *Graduation by exhibition: Assessing genuine achievement.* Arlington, VA: Association for Supervision and Curriculum Development.

Podl, J., & Metzger, M. (1992). *Anatomy of an exhibition.* Providence, RI: Coalition of Essential Schools. [Available from the Coalition for Essential Schools*]

About Projects

Goodrich, H., Hatch, T., Wiatrowski, G., & Unger, C. (1995). *Teaching through projects: Creating effective learning environments.* Menlo Park, CA: Addison Wesley.

Katz, L., & Chard, S. (1989). *Engaging children's minds: The project approach.* Norwood, NJ: Ablex.

Levy, S. (1996). *Starting from scratch: One classroom builds its own curriculum.* Portsmouth, NH: Heinemann.

Wigginton, E., & Students. (1991). *Foxfire: Twenty-five years.* New York: Anchor.

Winner, E., & Camp, R. (Eds.). (1992). *The Arts PROPEL handbooks* [a general handbook and one each for music, creative writing, and visual arts]. Cambridge, MA: Harvard Project Zero. [Available from Harvard Project Zero*]

About Portfolios

Defina, A. A. (1993). *Portfolio assessment: Getting started.* Jefferson City, MO: Scholastic. [Chapters 1–4 are especially relevant]

Hall, L., Stuart, L., & Engel, B. (1995). *The Cambridge handbook of documentation and assessment: Child portfolios and teacher records in the primary grades.* Grand Forks: University of North Dakota/North Dakota Study Group on Evaluation. [Available from the North Dakota Study Group*]

Jervis, K. (1996). *Eyes on the child: Three portfolio stories.* New York: Teachers College Press.

Lyons, N. (Ed.). (1998). *With portfolio in hand: Validating the new teacher professionalism.* New York: Teachers College Press.

Seidel, S., & Walters, J. (1994, December). The things children make in school: Disposable or indispensable? *Harvard Graduate School of Education Alumni Bulletin, 39* (1), 8–20.

Seidel, S., Walters, J., Kirby, E., Olff, N., Powell, K., Scripp, L., & Veenema, S. (1996). *Portfolio practices: Thinking through the assessment of student work.* Washington,

DC: NEA Publications Library. [Available from Harvard Project Zero*]

Winner, E. (Ed.). (1992). *The Arts PROPEL handbooks* [a general handbook and one each for music, creative writing, and visual arts]. Cambridge, MA: Harvard Project Zero. [Available from Harvard Project Zero*]

Wolf, D. P. (1989). Portfolio assessment: Sampling student work. *Educational Leadership, 46*(7), 35–39.

About Assessment (General)

Coalition of Essential Schools. (1995). *New York assessment collection* [Print and CD-ROM versions of a collection of exhibitions, portfolios, and performance tasks]. [Available from the Coalition of Essential Schools*]

Darling-Hammond, L., Ancess, J., & Falk, B. (1995). *Authentic assessment in action: Studies of schools and students at work.* New York: Teachers College Press.

Darling-Hammond, L., Einbender, L., Frelow, F., & Ley-King, J. (Eds.). (1993). *Authentic assessment in practice: A collection of portfolios, performance tasks, exhibitions, and documentation.* New York: Columbia University/NCREST. [Available from NCREST*]

Herman, J. L., Aschbacher, P. R., & Winters, L. (1992). *A practical guide to alternative assessment.* Alexandria, VA: Association for Supervision and Curriculum Development.

Johnson, B. (1996). *The performance assessment handbook, Vols. 1–2.* Princeton, NJ: Eye on Education. [Available from Eye on Education Press at (609) 395-0005]

Kornhaber, M., & Gardner, H. (1993). *Varieties of excellence: Identifying and assessing children's talents.* New York: Columbia University/NCREST. [Available from NCREST*]

Mitchell, R. (1992). *Testing for learning: How new approaches to evaluation can improve American schools.* New York: Free Press.

Newmann, F., Secada, W., & Wehlage, G. (1995). *A guide to authentic instruction and assessment: Vision, standards, and scoring.* Madison, WI: Wisconsin Center for Educational Research.

Northwest Regional Lab. *Assessment and accountability* [Page on the Northwest Regional Lab web site]. http://www.nwrel.org/eval/

Perrone, V. (1991). *Expanding student assessment.* Alexandria, VA: Association for Supervision and Curriculum Development.

Stiggins, R., & Conklin, N. F. (1992). *In teachers' hands: Investigating the practices of classroom assessment.* Albany: State University of New York Press.

Wiggins, G. (1993). *Assessing student performance: Exploring the purpose and limits of testing.* San Francisco: Jossey-Bass.

Wolf, D. P. (1988). Opening up assessment. *Educational Leadership, 45*, 24–29.

About Facilitating Groups

Howard, V. A., & Barton, J. H. (1992). *Thinking together: Making meetings work.* New York: William Morrow.

Perkins, D. N. (1994). *Missions in possibility space.* Unpublished manuscript, Harvard University/Project Zero. [Available from Harvard Project Zero*]

Organizations

For more information about the Collaborative Assessment Conference:

Harvard Project Zero
321 Longfellow Hall
Appian Way
Cambridge, MA 02138
(617) 495-4342
http:/+-9/pzweb.harvard.edu

For more information about the Tuning Protocol:

Annenberg Institute for School Reform
Brown University
Box 1985
Providence, RI 02912
(401) 863-7990
http://www.aisr.brown.edu

Coalition of Essential Schools
1814 Franklin Street
Oakland, CA 94612
(510) 433-1451
http://www.essentialschools.org

For information about Descriptive Review Processes:

Prospect Archive and Center for Education and Research
Box 326
North Bennington, VT 05257

For information about the Primary Language Record:

Centre for Language in Primary Education
Webber Row Teachers' Center
Webber Row
London SE1 8QW
http://www.rmplc.co.uk/orgs/clpe/

Center for Language in Learning
10610 Quail Canyon Road
El Cajon, CA 92021
(619) 443-6320
clrecord@cll.org

Additional organization addresses for obtaining materials:

NCREST
Box 110
Teachers College
Columbia University
New York, NY 10027
http://www.tc.columbia.edu/~ncrest

North Dakota Study Group
University of North Dakota
P.O. Box 7189
Grand Forks, ND 58202-7189

Website

The Looking at Student Work Website: http:// www.aisr.brown.edu/lsw

❖ About the Authors ❖

TINA BLYTHE is a researcher at Harvard Project Zero. She has taught middle and high school English in urban public schools. Her research has focused on instructional approaches that foster understanding, portfolio assessment, professional development, and whole school change. She is the principal author of *The Teaching for Understanding Guide* (Jossey-Bass, 1998).

DAVID ALLEN worked on this book as an associate at the Coalition of Essential Schools. He is currently a researcher at Harvard Project Zero. He has also worked for the Annenberg Institute for School Reform, Brown University. He has taught English and E.S.L. at the middle school, high school, and college levels. In 1996, he received a Fulbright research grant to study school reform in Poland. He is the editor of *Assessing Student Learning: From Grading to Understanding* (Teachers College Press, 1998).

BARBARA SCHIEFFELIN POWELL is an educational consultant to universities and schools. She was a classroom ethnographer for the Coalition of Essential Schools, Brown University, and the School Development Program at Yale University. She taught English and history in Blantyre, Malawi, and Newton, MA public schools. She has been a high school principal and has taught at Wellesley College, Harvard University, and the University of Bielefeld, Germany. A recent publication is *Toward Understanding* (Annenberg Institute for School Reform, 1998).

KATHLEEN CUSHMAN is a Senior Associate of the Annenberg Institute and of the Coalition of Essential Schools. She is the writer and editor of *Horace*, a publication of the Coalition of Essential Schools. She has been actively involved in the founding and operation of the Francis W. Parker Charter School in Fort Devens, MA.